Invisible Insane

Afric McGlinchey

SV

SurVision Books

First published in 2019 by
SurVision Books
Dublin, Ireland
www.survisionmagazine.com

Copyright © Afric McGlinchey, 2019

Cover image © Cian Hamilton, 2019

Design © SurVision Books, 2019

ISBN: 978-1-9995903-3-8

This book is in copyright. No part of this publication may be reproduced, stored in a retrieval system, or transmitted in any form or by any means without the prior permission in writing from the publisher.

Acknowledgements

Grateful acknowledgement is made to the editors of the following, in which a number of these poems, or their versions, originally appeared:

Banshee, Big River Review, Crannóg, Headstuff, Numéro Cinq; Poethead, Prelude, Rochford Street Review, Tears in the Fence, The Brain of Forgetting, The Ofi Magazine, The Stinging Fly, Valve.

A version of *Body Notes* (formerly titled *The Ignorance of Fish*) was commended in the Oxford University Sci-Po competition, 2018.

The poet also wishes to express sincere gratitude to the Arts Council of Ireland for awarding a bursary in 2018.

'Invisible insane' is Google Translate's Japanese version of the English proverb: *'out of sight, out of mind.'*

CONTENTS

On the Quay of Flames	5
The Green Taste of Youth	6
Cha	7
Human	8
While the Sleepers	9
After the Blossoming, Boom	10
Rabblement	11
More than Skin	12
Third Law	13
Body Notes	14
Living Proof	16
Particle of Light through a Raindrop	17
A Travelling Country of Windows	18
Silver Wings	19
Whose Territory	20
Viewpoint	21
Base	22
Invisible Insane	23
Anomie	24
The Sea's Dream	25
The Speed of Life	26
Into the Iron Winter	27
The Thing with Feathers	28
End of the Blessing	29
As Pearl Cat Catches Rain	30

On the Quay of Flames

The small heir blithely bypassed the world,
staked his post to the republic of dreams,
screwing together the boards of the first living library.

On the side, two tongues, not an overcoat stranger,
something more fluid: water poured into a vase.
A footing of sinuous little replicas, twisted

into place at 5 o'clock. On the quay of flames,
the limping man drew tiny, counter Xs.
At the turn of the untilled field, his discovery:

a pure tapestry, transposition of estrangement,
resting on adopted terrain.
In rejection, there is luck.

See what happens. Leave the second stone,
turn up curios: the cosmic breath
of a soul, taking sideways form.

Preternatural alterities lurk within
furniture, gloomy canopies. They step not twice,
but endlessly into a wavy river, mingle as one.

Nostalgia is restorative. In any case,
experience the effect.
Plainly see the first day of the world.

The Green Taste of Youth

is a summer carousel, horses playing
arson, burning stables

without restraint or hold-alls
for the new world.

In the tower, light is bared
and swinging, laughing manically.

Unlatch your tongue, paint
it with saliva, spill any random

words, and spin, poi split-
time butterflies

Cha

after All My Friends,
a song composed and performed by Edan Ray

Nearly ran to the riptide confluence.
Only you know the notion of if.
Only you rush into the pedal of music,
crossovers smacking up against the wayward torques
in liquid and you and you and you, my friends,
run backwards into all the peripheral stories,
slow motion as the ocean. Shhh... or bass it.
Only you keep me laughing. Strobe-light-
fix each gesture in distortion,
loose-wristed, star-fired, brainless
with excitement. Cha.

Human

The fact that you're rolling
downhill like a Cuban cigar
in your sleeping bag, to land
jammed up next to mine,
makes your grass journey a genius act.
The skies cocoon so many phantoms.
Twenty cheers for the first kiss,
the move to a lucky tent
that requires only starlight
for a hibiscus-pink performance.
We are a million nights, a fox hairbrush.
Before you eat the cake, I Instagram it.
Your shoulders flex and reflex.
Trains are a slow noise,
bicycles, the acquisition of holy music.
Someone or nothing catches
a catacomb of moods.
Glass perhaps, between hallucinations.

While the Sleepers

The muse in the field
is a pop-up book.
His bed is a tongue
of grass. I am who.

I will press my finger into
the bowl of the muse's body,
place some of his dusty fire
over my eyelids.

Instead of idling
in pyjamas, I'll go
door-to-door with the dawn,
one sunrise at a time.

After the Blossoming, Boom
for Sara Baume

The raised voices of summer
petals engage, like birds,
in public relations,
contiguous with the glare
and nerves of the sun,
the scraping of chairs
and the gaping of mouths.
Alice sees through the gaps,
of course, and substitutions:
pig for fig or bird for human,
while Baume reads post-
humous feathers and snouts, still
at their barre-work, heraldic
as Godard when the race is done.

Rabblement

Wildly, can't find language enough.
Each week, some scissors
redacting the feelings that make us up.
Textual complexity is too much
for a newspaper's
*Korean woman found dead
in direct provision centre*

So left of *press for mum*, even
in fragments.
There must be wind,
because the leaves are tossing,
but I can't hear it
as the window won't recognise
the word to *open*;

A six-year-old Korean child
doesn't know he's hungry
hasn't eaten since this rubbish
crushed his mother,
who made the only choice she could
and now no amount of wind
will wake the leaves

More than Skin

after Frida Kahlo

Among cacti phalli
where you hold court,
an uproar of falling towers.

Dark skin floats to light,
lavish as radishes
among lush leaves.

You drown pain,
escape by tightrope,
flamenco.

Your Judas bones, a frame
for the spiralling weave,
heart of your art.

Twenty red-tipped
toes –
wings in flight.

Third Law

The slow, hurting body
of the planet is undulating
in sulphur yellow,
red aposematic.
It's not enough to say it once.
Creativity, like realism,
has always been magic.
Say it five times.
A swan with a punctured eye
turns its head and *sings terribly, afar,*
in the lost lands.
Put your moth mask on
and rainbow like the stardust particles of Bjork,
like languid half dancers
swallowing hyper objects
in a world without skin.
To say it.
We are meshing with Styrofoam,
with the habitats of the dead.
Say it.
What will outlast the speech bubble?
This is the time of error.
The snow globe is filling with plutonium,
psychically cracked.
Five times.
We are wading up to our knees in toxic water.
Creativity is not enough.

Body Notes

I

Fish swim, oblivious of song
until their body leaves water.
Think of fish sailing
through air, while Lyric
is playing Dvořák.
Think of a pipefish wheel,
watching cumulus journeys.
Cloud on the body of sky.

II

The tall hill is layered with trees,
sun bolting to red.
Think of a rocket, a blaze.
Soldiers on the horizon.
Think of the rack of bodies
as a war machine.
Think of the rhythm of truth
as the rhythm of ricochet.

III

The room is a suitcase
and does not belong to the doll.
The walls are a swallow of blood.
The stigmata is female.
Think of the notes of her bones.
Think of the pit; think of descent.
This is otherness. Sometimes
the body whimpers.

IV

The tongue is the keeper of flame,
especially when singing.
Think of tone as a swooning.
Nakedness is intuitive.
Think of light through a dream.
Now a body is unlocking a door,
spilling a cup,
blooming with scales.

Living Proof

You make wet collodion tintypes
that heap paddle-shaped rain-spill
pulling itself together
across plaited curves of clay.
Those knotted clouds in its mirror
barely keep still long enough
for me to be certain of their broken-eyed faces.
An elongated tree grows outside the frame,
thin as vinegar,
its limbs almost ready to ascend into heaven.
Your head, a fat bell,
rocks back and forth, as if tolling.
Savage coat un-blending from the shadows;
such a vexed beast, all that redundant knowing.

Particle of Light through a Raindrop

If houses are lifted up and dropped, like crystal,
then shards cutting through memory.

If the cat swims, ears and nose above water,
then arms reaching to rescue.

If you hold my hand, though I feel it empty,
then rain, landing on earth and soaking it anyway.

If sun bursts from the sky, un-bedding the fog,
then, without coat, without hat, armour for a new journey.

A Travelling Country of Windows

All the bony roads,
spokes shaking off a mouthful
of sleet, and you
further forward than me, or inward perhaps
– a heaped bush – stop.
I know what is in that box
stiffly packaged in white canvas
– the first of the seven sorrows –
then the next to come tumbling
will be – no, let's
travel back, round the coastline up north
where the mattress groaned under
our bouncing feet and feathers flew
from the bolsters, until the creak
of a door, pink glow of the landing wallpaper.
And fast as the smallest
laughing fury, we're under the sheets:
one on the floor, pretend-sleeping,
a silence lunging from above.
Imagine it's tipping its point
like a Damacles sword.
Fleeting shock;
and then the rattling again,
struggling past the cages.

Silver Wings

You recognise someone saying your name,
and you go right up to the moment,
right up to the third person within you,
but they're a different shape
in some essential way,
and you re-read your traces,
like a tree stroking
its silver wings against the wind
a tree in the cold,
a tree its own breath.

Whose Territory

By the shaded tree,
all the boulders keeping secrets.
Deeper than a tent,
the boy waits until their backs are turned.
He says they're not as sealed as they seem to be.
Let's try pitchforks, mowers, magic wands.
Those boulders are like milk. They're liquid – drink them up,
Now try archery.

He enlists the use of natural forces when he's making love,
all pine, while I am apple, playing delectable.
There's no god taking us by the scruff of the neck,
but in the lightning storm, everything turns fugitive.
I want to know the mind of hunters,
yelping dogs who get the rabbits out of hiding.
And another thing.
Tripping into the dark, the boundless.

Viewpoint

How quiet the rioting
beyond revolving doors.
Which the liar, ears or eyes?
We raise our brows,
bewildered by the tension.
See this serrated knife?
I lay it on the palest of the plates,
wait for your disapproval.
Will you cut?
Ever closer, their breath,
its volume broad as night.
A trillion pico-seconds
cluster in a glass-thin
slice. You frame it.

Base

A hardening, salt on the fences, wire cutters, whistling freedom. And the sky is ironic laughter. So hard for the mind to fix beyond murals of armed men. Fireworks, kerb stones, honey and crystals. Merge into wall in Belfast. Twisting ribbons between each barrier, dissolving concrete with rain. The crossing of borders; cut to check-points, toxic-routes through all the back gardens. So black and blue. Walls begin farther, all the way to Berlin, louder again, more reverberant. Punching out holes or hurdling, placing totems around all the bases. This is base.

Invisible Insane

It was always the other way round.
           – Margaret Atwood

Not up against a wall,
your three-legged
mind

jaywalking across
my shadow, or the city's
muddled roundabouts.

Not merging our reflections
in a winter window,
laughing at the idea

of our planet
being a snow globe
for the angels.

No matter
where, there's
no getting you

out of my mind.
Are you google
earthing me?

Is that you
I can hear, between
bells, faintly?

Anomie

The old philosopher, sharp as ice.
Our thinking (not upright as trees,
 as we thought) is fractured by his voice.

His words conflate human agency
with the natural order,
the body of shared memory

with the vanished sign.
There should be flowers, he tells us,
in a clear-cut voice, simple as ink.

Every night, his teachings
turn to the blue laws,
or stallions, or the Book of Hours.

He invites invocation or,
at least, resistance,
to those overpouring thoughts

that have taken us down
an avenue lined
with little lamps of snow.

The Sea's Dream

The sea's dream is the ship
moving with the sun
along the indigo-edge of a child's stick horizon.

The sea's dream is the ship
fleeing an hourglass,
watched by the albatross overhead, silently.

The ship traces an ocean planet,
over the ballet of manta ray and slow-falling fish,
underwater flights from equator to pole.

The ship bends into a street of moonlight,
invites travellers to kiss
the sea's shrinking reflection

unfold vestigial gills and fly
down, down, down to the sea's secret garden,
our older memory.

The Speed of Life

King kongs, bottle washers, genies,
are lifted to colour air, light as glass.
Doors disappear down dwarf alley.
The marvellous boy drinking dam-cooled beer
knows that bees are few,
just as the boat-man knows a boat's emotions,
and the wind knows that it's tired, yet still braces wings
for nine last strokes of havoc.
We walk on scarred and scraggy knees
through the gates of memory,
its silence leaching away the day, the decades,
until we are in a graveyard lake of detritus,
its unkind wave chasing. We face spent grief,
empty our pockets, surrender.

Into the Iron Winter

sky just a body
dreaming of poppies,
silver fish

trees stare across water
towards laughter,
soft as blue moss

a mother's thin, white cup
notes her hands
around its small planet

memory
opens
its long window

hidden stars,
wind in the door,
tail in the alley

between shadows and dirt,
a girl lifts an apple
feels a bird turn

The Thing with Feathers

Beneath the vaulting, kneeling
and kyphotic, she rocks, a pendulum.

In each radiating chapel, a candle
forest is offered up to souls.

The choir's complex harmonics echo
across pews. Incense is a series

of hovering exhalations, visible
as umbrellas in the narthex.

Prayers flutter, three
hundred breaths a minute.

Lungs, rain-licked,
hum white; each tongue

an edelweiss. Leadlight
vignettes glitter

in the clerestory: an angel's
wing-lashed fire,

in twenty-one-gram
refractions, holding all this.

End of the Blessing

To me you were the heart's X
against my Guernica wall,
drowning out calamity.

I was addicted to your trip trap
words, lush as ferns,
all the way to fractal.

And the tandoor of my body grew
wide awake; tongue, a fire
racing through the field.

You seduced my mind,
till it was perpetually
undressed.

What's left inside me, now
you've drifted off,
taking all the alleluias?

As Pearl Cat Catches Rain

as pearl cat catches rain, air draws cloud
to land on street in handfuls

and cobbles sing; each whispered drop
spells helter-skelter pin-head,

in a dream-extending glimmer
as each living creature lives one life

and a similar; sleep goes waking itself,
charms the happenstance of when;

and this: a catcall sings a metronome; takes two
million pieces through your eyes, other places.

More poetry published by SurVision Books

Noelle Kocot. *Humanity*
(New Poetics: USA)
ISBN 978-1-9995903-0-7

Ciaran O'Driscoll. *The Speaking Trees*
(New Poetics: Ireland)
ISBN 978-1-9995903-1-4

Helen Ivory. *Maps of the Abandoned City*
(New Poetics: England)
ISBN 978-1-912963-04-1

Elin O'Hara Slavick. *Cameramouth*
(New Poetics: USA)
ISBN 978-1-9995903-4-5

John W. Sexton. *Inverted Night*
(New Poetics: Ireland)
ISBN 978-1-912963-05-8

George Kalamaras. *That Moment of Wept*
ISBN 978-1-9995903-7-6

Anton Yakovlev. *Chronos Dines Alone*
(Winner of James Tate Poetry Prize 2018)
ISBN 978-1-912963-01-0

Bob Lucky. *Conversation Starters in the Language No One Speaks*
(Winner of James Tate Poetry Prize 2018)
ISBN 978-1-912963-00-3

Christopher Prewitt. *Paradise Hammer*
(Winner of James Tate Poetry Prize 2018)
ISBN 978-1-9995903-9-0

Mikko Harvey & Jake Bauer. *Idaho Falls*
(Winner of James Tate Poetry Prize 2018)
ISBN 978-1-912963-02-7

Anatoly Kudryavitsky. *Stowaway*
(New Poetics: Ireland)
ISBN 978-1-9995903-2-1

Maria Grazia Calandrone. *Fossils*
Translated from Italian
(New Poetics: Italy)
ISBN 978-1-9995903-6-9

Sergey Biryukov. *Transformations*
Translated from Russian
(New Poetics: Russia)
ISBN 978-1-9995903-5-2

Alexander Korotko. *Irrazionalismo*
Translated from Russian
(New Poetics: Ukraine)
ISBN 978-1-912963-06-5

Anton G. Leitner. *Selected Poems 1981–2015*
Translated from German
ISBN 978-1-9995903-8-3

Our books are available to order via
http://survisionmagazine.com/books.htm

www.ingramcontent.com/pod-product-compliance
Lightning Source LLC
Chambersburg PA
CBHW071958060426
42444CB00043B/2650